Look After Yourself

Look After Yourself

Your Body

Claire Llewellyn

W

FRANKLIN WATTS
LONDON • SYDNEY

This edition 2004

Franklin Watts
96 Leonard Street
London
EC2A 4XD

Franklin Watts Australia
45-51 Huntley Street
Alexandria
NSW 2015

Copyright © Franklin Watts 2002

Series editor: Sarah Peutrill
Art director: Jonathan Hair
Design: Kirstie Billingham
Illustrations: James Evans
Photographs: Ray Moller unless otherwise acknowledged
Picture research: Diana Morris
Series consultant: Lynn Huggins-Cooper

Acknowledgments:
Biophoto Associates/SPL: 23tr
Layne Kennedy/Corbisstockmarket: 19
Brian Mitchell/Photofusion: 23bl

With thanks to our models: Aaron, Charlotte, Connor, Jake, Holly and Nadine

A CIP record for this book is available from the British Library.

Dewey Classification 613

ISBN: 0 7496 5648 4

Printed in Hong Kong/China

Contents

Looking after yourself

Think of all the things your body does - it speaks, moves, grows, feels and breathes. Your body works hard all the time.
It's important to look after it.

Your body never stops working.

What is your body doing right now?

When we are very young, we can't look after ourselves. Our parents do it for us.

This boy is too young to look after himself.

This girl can brush her own hair.

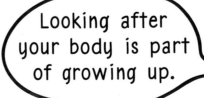

As we grow older, we can do more. We learn to wash our face and brush our hair. This is part of growing up.

Looking after your body is part of growing up.

Keeping clean

You need to have a wash when you get up in the morning. A good wash helps you to wake up.

Wash your face every morning.

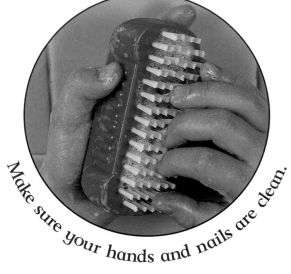

Make sure your hands and nails are clean.

During the day your body works all the time. Your skin becomes warm and sweaty, and if you don't wash the sweat away you will begin to smell.

In the evening you need a good wash, or a bath or shower to wash your skin clean.

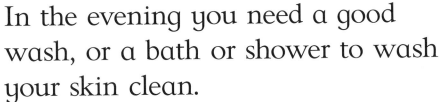

Who wants to be smelly? Not me!

Mmm! Clean people smell great.

Water with soap, shower gel or bubble bath helps to keep us clean. What do you use?

Make sure you rinse all the soap away. Then carefully dry yourself all over with a towel.

Wash away germs

Every part of your body gets dirty.
It's important to keep it clean.
Washing helps to get rid of germs.

There are germs in the air around us.

What are germs?

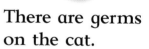

There are germs on the cat.

Germs are tiny living things in the world around us. You can't see them, but they are everywhere - on the things we touch and in the air around us.

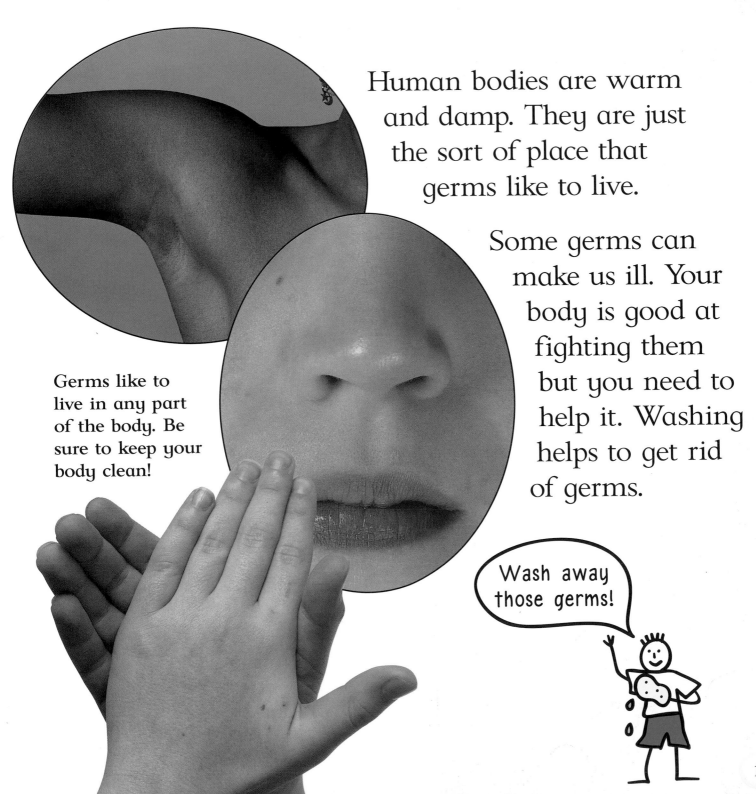

Human bodies are warm and damp. They are just the sort of place that germs like to live.

Some germs can make us ill. Your body is good at fighting them but you need to help it. Washing helps to get rid of germs.

Germs like to live in any part of the body. Be sure to keep your body clean!

Wash away those germs!

Teeth, hair and nails

Some parts of your body need extra care.
It is important to look after your teeth.
Some foods can harm them and make
them decay. When that happens, your
breath starts to smell and in time your teeth
will hurt. Brushing helps to protect them.

Brush your teeth after breakfast
and before you go to bed.

Clean teeth
give you a
nice smile!

Hair needs washing at least once or twice a week. Some people wash their hair every day! This washes the dirt away and keeps it smooth and shiny.

Cut your nails carefully or ask someone to help you.

Germs live under our fingernails. We need to keep them clean. It's best to have your nails cut short. Then they don't get so dirty.

Short nails are easier to keep clean.

Germs can spread

Germs can spread from one person to another.
They can make you sick, upset your tummy,
or give you a cough or cold.

Coughs and colds are spread
by germs. How do you
feel when you have
a cold?

Washing your hands can stop germs spreading. Wash them with soap before you touch any food and after you go to the toilet.

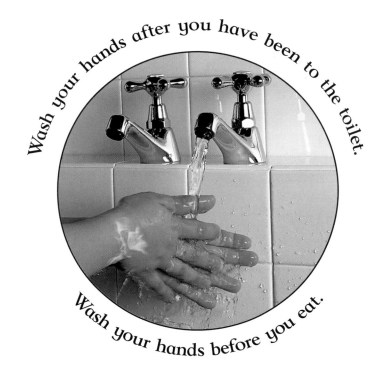

Wash your hands after you have been to the toilet.

Wash your hands before you eat.

Use a hanky when you sneeze. This traps germs in your handkerchief and stops them spreading through the air.

Atishoo! Always catch your sneeze in a hanky.

A healthy diet

There are other ways you can look after your body. The food you eat is very important. Different foods help the body in different ways.

These foods give you energy.

These help you to fight germs and stay healthy.

How many different foods have you eaten today?

These help your body to grow and mend itself.

Make sure your body gets everything it needs by eating many different kinds of food. This is called a healthy diet.

Are there any foods I shouldn't eat?

Sweetcorn is delicious and good for you too!

No food is bad for you, but try not to eat too many sugary foods. Sugar harms your teeth.

Sugary foods rot your teeth. Only eat them now and then.

Keeping fit

Exercise is very good for the body. Our bodies don't like to sit down all the time.
They like to get up and go!

Phew! Skipping is a great way to keep fit.

Exercise can be a lot of fun, especially with your friends.

Exercise is good for you in many different ways. It makes your muscles bigger and your bones stronger. It makes your heart beat faster and your lungs work harder. It helps to keep you fit!

Look at my muscles!

What do you like to do?

There are lots of different ways to keep fit.

A good rest

Our bodies like to exercise, but they also need to rest. By the end of the day, they begin to slow down. We begin to feel more and more tired.

Sometimes it's hard to stay awake.
What time do you go to bed?

I'm too tired to read my book.

It is important to have a good night's sleep.
Sleep rests every part of your body. It gives
you the energy you'll need tomorrow.
It helps to make you as good as new.

Mmm!
I love my bed –
it's so cosy.

Your body
needs plenty
of rest. How
many hours
do you sleep
every night?

On the mend

Our bodies get bumped and bruised all the time. The body is good at mending itself, but you can give it a helping hand. If you cut or graze your skin, it needs to be washed clean.

The cut will soon begin to heal. Your body seals it with a scab so germs can't get inside.

This knee has a nasty graze.

Never pick at scabs! The germs on your fingers can get into the cut and infect it! The scab will fall off when the skin has healed.

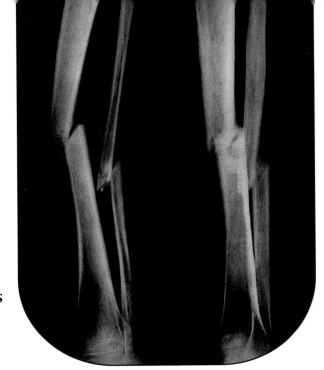

Can you see where the bones are broken in this x-ray?

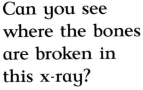

Did you know that if you break a bone, it mends all by itself? A doctor puts the bone inside a plaster cast, so that it grows back straight and strong. It takes six to eight weeks for a bone to mend.

This girl has a plaster cast on her broken arm. She also has a sling to support it.

Feeling ill

We all feel ill from time to time.
When you are ill it's a good idea to stay in bed.
Sleep helps your body to mend itself.

Resting is important at times like these. It helps the body to fight the illness.

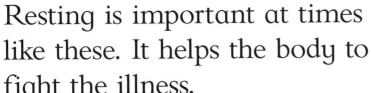

Sometimes we need to see a doctor. Doctors understand how the body works. They can help us to get better.

Keeping safe

Doctors sometimes have to give us medicines. Medicines are very strong. We need to use them carefully. It's important for a grown-up to give you your medicine - never take it on your own!

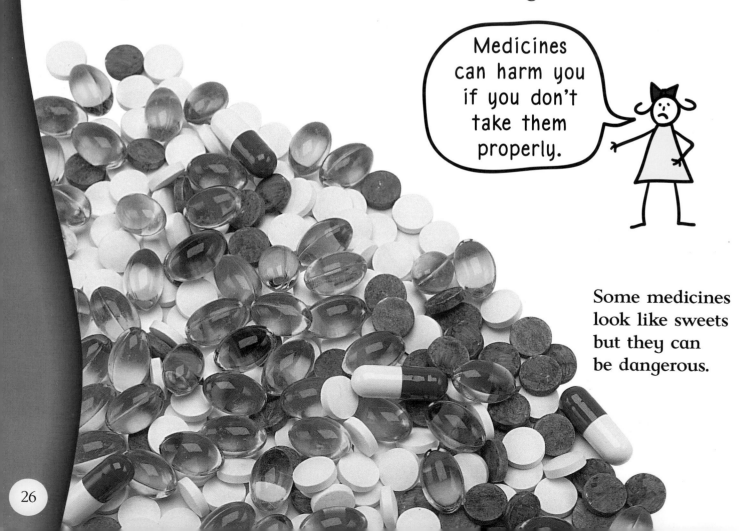

Medicines can harm you if you don't take them properly.

Some medicines look like sweets but they can be dangerous.

Other things in the home can be dangerous, too – such as cleaners, paints and glues. Never touch, sniff or swallow things like this. They could harm you.

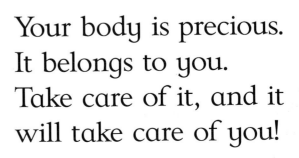

Grown-ups keep dangerous things locked away, and in high cupboards!

Always look after your body.

Your body is precious. It belongs to you. Take care of it, and it will take care of you!

Glossary

dangerous   something that could hurt you

diet   the food and drink that you usually eat

doctor   a person whose job is to try and make sick people get better

energy   the power we get from food, which makes us able to work and grow, and keep warm

exercise   to be active

germs   tiny living things that can spread disease and make you feel ill. Germs are too small to see

graze   when you scrape your skin on something hard

hanky   also called a handerkerchief. A square of cloth to blow your nose on

healthy   fit and well

illness something that makes you feel unwell

medicine a liquid or tablet that you take when you are ill.

plaster cast something that is wrapped around a broken bone to help it to heal

rot when something goes bad

scab a hard crust that covers a cut or graze while it is healing

sugar something that is found in many foods and makes them taste sweet

sweat a liquid that comes out of your skin when your body is hot

tooth decay when teeth go bad and have holes in them

x-ray a special photograph that shows the bones inside you

Index

About this book

Learning the principles of how to keep healthy and clean is one of life's most important skills. **Look After Yourself** is a series aimed at young children who are just beginning to develop these skills. **Your Body** looks at cleanliness and keeping the body healthy.

Here are a number of activities that children could try:

Pages 6-7 Discuss all the things they can do on their own. How much has changed since they were babies?

Pages 8-9 Test some different soaps and shower gels. Which creates a lather most quickly? Which has the nicest smell?

Pages 10-11 Make a poster to explain the ways we can avoid germs.

Pages 12-13 If appropriate, look at and test different nail scissors and cutters. Which is the easiest to use?

Pages 14-15 Write about the last time they were poorly. How did they feel? What and who helped them to get better?

Pages 16-17 Write a menu for one day. Make sure it contains a variety of foods from all the food groups.

Pages 18-19 Devise and play some games with friends that use lots of energy. Afterwards, decide which game was the most tiring. Why?

Pages 20-21 Find out how many hours of sleep different people in a family get. Who has the most sleep? Who has the least? Discuss why this is.

Pages 22-23 Discuss why cuts, grazes and other accidents can be painful - the body is warning that something is wrong.

Pages 24-25 Make a list of all the qualities a doctor needs. Which is the most important?

Pages 26-27 Discuss where we get medicines from (i.e the chemist).